Free Verse Editions
Edited by Jon Thompson

THE CALLING

Bruce Bond

Parlor Press
Anderson, South Carolina
www.parlorpress.com

Parlor Press LLC, Anderson, South Carolina, 29621

© 2021 by Parlor Press
All rights reserved.
Printed in the United States of America
S A N: 2 5 4 - 8 8 7 9

Library of Congress Cataloging-in-Publication Data on File

978-1-64317-152-4 (paperback)
978-1-64317-153-1 (pdf)
978-1-64317-154-8 (ePub)

1 2 3 4 5

Cover image: Vilhelm Hammershøi, "Woman Seen from the Back." Oil on canvas. 1888. National Gallery of Denmark. Used by permission.

Cover design by David Blakesley.

Parlor Press, LLC is an independent publisher of scholarly and trade titles in print and multimedia formats. This book is available in paperback and ebook formats from Parlor Press on the World Wide Web at http://www.parlorpress.com or through online and brick-and-mortar bookstores. For submission information or to find out about Parlor Press publications, write to Parlor Press, 3015 Brackenberry Drive, Anderson, South Carolina, 29621, or email editor@parlorpress.com.

CONTENTS

Each word for *Muslim* or *boy* or *bloodline* now. It lies
   across another.   *5*
The one who names is nameless and one   *6*
When I say *wind*, I see leaves and call them *wind*.   *7*
This is a story that ends in a desert landscape   *9*
The sun that dissolves the names of the rivers, it lifts
   them up.   *11*
Cruelty understands so little of its object,   *12*
Everything we see arrives a little late.   *13*

II. *15*

You can hear the tremor of the ouds of ancient Morocco   *17*
Music is quick, lithe, incisive as a bullet,   *18*
The gun that takes the elephant down,   *19*
Long ago the signature of the Lydian ascension   *20*
The trumpet lies down with the daylight in its casket   *21*
Beneath the bells and tremors of the tower, all the angels
   are kids,   *22*
To each the silence   *23*
The other side of lamentation is the shape it makes.   *24*

III. *27*

Every voice an epitaph, and then a little tune   *29*
The girl who clings to her mother's skirt at the
   polling station   *30*
In his final year, my father grew tomatoes. He knelt   *31*
Every night   *32*
One day   *33*
I am searching my ballot for the nameless.   *34*
The light that leaves the body in the morning,   *35*
When I gather what the nameless left,   *36*
I read it in an old book: *37*

Contents

IV. *39*

    I carry a face *41*
    And if one I knew and loved should feed *42*
    And I will wonder *43*
    Is the cry a cry *44*
    When the answer cannot be put in words, neither can
        the question be put in words. *45*

V. *47*

    The passports of the tombstones *49*
    As a child I learned and forgot and learned again *50*
    Bidden or unbidden, God abideth. So says the tomb *51*
    Bidden or unbidden, dream visits the sleepless man, *52*
    I have a friend who lost the memory of a year from
        his childhood, *53*
    The smell of smoke and roses in a bar, *54*
    To every infant, the daze of arrival. *55*
    There is the silence of abundance and that of abandon, *56*
    Out of nothing, the fire of affluence and that of ruin. *57*

Acknowledgments *59*
About the Author *61*
Free Verse Editions *63*

*I opened my mouth
and a small part of the void, which filled
the early morning street and nearby houses, entered me.*

— Tomasz Różycki

The Calling

I.

Each word for *Muslim* or *boy* or *bloodline* now. It lies across another.
    And the body wears the mask
                of a thousand words
        it does not understand.

                A certain skin keeps me here.
Me here. You there.
                If it does not breathe.
                It dies.
                If it does not hold me.

Who has not tried to explain themselves
and fallen deeper in confusion.

Pinch me, I say, when I get bewildered,
but all I feel is skin.

Me here. You there. I am always in the way. Call me, *Muslim*.
    And my name lies down
    in a Muslim's grave.

The light that masks the many in a photograph
                        is the light of the room
                        that holds the picture.
            This room

        lies down
        in the darkened glass.

All of us now in one bell of light
                      that tolls for the many.

The one who names is nameless and one
          in the sense of wind as one
  before the limbs, dismantling the long path,

    break their truce with silence.

The one who writes the story,
     she is in there, out there, somewhere

         in the news she would make
   clear as camera glass

  before the jeeps of the militia arrive to smash it.

And say the camera keeps rolling. And you see everything
   through a shatter. You see

the camera as the eye of someone nameless still.
   The smoke in the streets,
     it lingers
    for a week. Maybe two.

  The blue metal in the air.

When the vision leaves, the scent remains. When the journalist
  vanishes, her column

    tells the story of her vanishing.
We add her name to the nameless whose stories are too many.
   We name her *here*.
        You *there*.

    When I say *wind*, I see leaves and call them *wind*.
        The one in many it cannot be.

I see the smoke of a thousand refugees
                      pour across the border.

In every ocean lies another, smaller, deeper.
          In every body, water, salt.

    In every failure at sea, the silent wreckage of the floor.

Today I learned a ship was taken down
                    with the names in a ledger
    that no one reads.
    And our name for this is *refugee*.

                Who, what, why, when your home
is on fire and your nation rivers to the open sea.

In every bloodstream the fine and finer details of the blood.
    The core of us is strange,

      and when we read, a stranger reads:
                    this skin,

    it is not the movie. It is the screen.

And when you read the movie, the skin remains.

                      Untouched.

   Take this bloodline, and a thousand strangers
pour across the border, and sometimes what follows is remorse,
      bitterness, smoke,

       and I who speak something
  of their language
  know nothing of their names.

  Those left behind, they talk to the camera.
  A boy steadies his arm for the bandage,
          and the words

float out.

    And you see in his eye the shatter of a stranger.
  The world with pieces of glass in it.

        Bits of eye.

    In this way the damage transcends
    any one home
    invasion or bullet
    stripped of its jacket.

    Clean and gag the wound to heal it.

    And still, as the boy falls asleep,
    the blood continues. The bandage blooms.

This is a story that ends in a desert landscape
                with stones
       where people lay their flowers.

With skin that is spiritually
             scared, scarred, speechless.

                And every bullet bears its name.

      This is a story that a story tells itself.
      And the sound of it is speechless.

                The wound that opens its eye in the dark,

it sees the red there.

              Beneath the skin.

   Every body bears its name.

              And as it heals, it goes
              blind. And as the fire
              on the threshold fades:

       the clarity of dark.

Sometimes a shock so great, it shakes the person from her body.

    And she might talk about it, and the talking helps,
        some.

A little language leaves the flesh that speaks and looks back
    as if to say, know:
    I have not forgotten you.

        I call you mine. Again.
        And I am talking to a beast
            and frightened of my voice.

I want to say, I know. I understand. It is my animal nature.
    I have not forgotten my nameless homeland.

Those who raise livestock, they too understand: to name an animal
        as you would a child

    makes the slaughter impossible
                      to bear.

And you want to say something to someone. To get
    over it. To get it
    right. (I have not forgotten you.)

        And then, being human, you want it
        less and less.

The sun that dissolves the names of the rivers, it lifts them up.

    It reveals. Enlightens.
    Someone told me a parable once.

    A meditation on the mercy of disenfranchisement.

    How the core of us is nameless.
        And yes. It is.

    How the wound is an eye—yes—

            that opens—yes—on a context of stars
    whose assignations vanish in the fire.

And my body replied, But a wound, named or unnamed,
    is a wound.

        I was thinking of the parable
      where the one patrol car enters the smoke

    of the warehouse district and lo,
it turns into a thousand,
      and every license bears the signature,
          nameless,
            and every face
a mask of light
      from the unseen fire

          crackling on the shore.

Cruelty understands so little of its object,
        its object is no object.
        No subject either.

I cannot know this.
         And maintain a spell of power
    as particular, fixed, named, and thereby
      blind.

The man, winged and bleeding in the target, is always missed.

To the eye that shoots the blot of ink in the crosshair,
      there is no man.

And then, in his vanishing, there is.

If I tell my story to the river,
        and the river rises, if I confess
across the blotter of the man at the station,
          it does not mean
I understand.
If I turn the way the widow turns to the glass of the clock

      and see the face
      around the eye that sees,

      the clarity of a missing eye,
    the bullet of sight
         passing through.

        Everything we see arrives a little late.
                        The news is never new.

    Everything we see, each dead star
               in a sky of stars, touches an eye it cannot
touch.

This uneasiness in these trees, it comes
        from a place so far away no landscape can explain.

Night lies down in the word for *night*,
    and when I wake, a footprint dries
            at the water's edge
                    where an animal bowed to
drink.

Every explanation has a landscape in it.

          When I say *I*, there is more than one
   speaker, reader, face to read, more
             than one blinded by a face.

When I hold my passport out
          and the guard checks my photo, my race,
my nation,

    I act innocent,
        which is to say, suspicious. I look him in the eye.
        I speak.
           And never quite cross over.

II.

You can hear the tremor of the ouds of ancient Morocco

    in the distant cousin, the Spanish guitar,

                                and the Moor in the
morning
        prayer, the djembe in the snap of the dancer's fan,

the vihuela in the viola, you hear the plectrum in the word
        oud, whose echo *lute*
    you hear in some girl's voice
        in Northern Europe, and the Babylonian

chordophone whose name we lost, you hear its music
    in an old stone engraving, because spirit does that,

it cuts the stone away, music dies into music and the new there cuts you
    open, you hear the sternum

        of the instrument shiver because we make it
light, strong, we break it in, you hear

    the high pitches of the medical machine,
as the patient sleeps, and the bad heart is lifted from its chamber,

    the harvest of the other,
        fresh from the cooler, lies down in the dark
warm pit,

    and the man who receives, he told his child once:
the Iron Age gave us our own word Yah,
        that lies in turn in the Hebrew alleluia,

and about now the boy in the chorus, he is wondering if his father will survive,

    and if you listen hard, he is in there still,
        the child as the father of the music he becomes.

       Music is quick, lithe, incisive as a bullet,
                               however slow the measure.

Out of the wound the gut the throat the horn the little dish

                of ashes at the table,

through the chatter of the glasses
        and bottles on the wall   and into the street

      where a boy is playing a shiny trumpet made of air,
      music arrives a little early. Nameless, new, unrepentant.

And the song is blue as the day is hot, which is why he plays it,

because some days the beauty in the sky in the barbed fields of cotton
        hurts,

                             and the music gets it,
           gets oddly specific
where there are no words, no *Louisiana* yet, no coin
                             of the realm.

Whatever the passage, it is changing hands, because, to hell with that
        and that, it says,
               and the strange new hand on another's arm
is here and gone and here again, changed again and slightly more at
home.

And the horns are growing
        brighter, bolder.

        And the smoke in a woman's body
                             is breaking into laughter.

    The gun that takes the elephant down,
                the roar of the great beneficent beast

and the dust that rises, the slave
            who saws through the cream
                      of the ivory, the five men
bought to carry, the one in five who dies of exhaustion, the roar

    of the great beneficent wind and the spume it raises,
        the long sea journey, the one in five
                  ships chained to the dead who go
down with it, the look of the drowned
            in the living, the open eye of the departed,

        the song of the wreck
                on the ocean floor:

they are bound, all of them, for the grand pianos of Europe,

            where a composer, an insomniac,
beaten as a child, a solitary man,
    a nervous temper and a hair-storm in his prime,
        will lay his fingers on the white keys,
                    whose names dissolve,
        because he is just that full

of some vague demand, something he forgot as a boy and never did remember.

And the long legacy
    will pull one direction, written, and the music another,
        and the oceans will erase

                the deep engravings of the shore.

     Long ago the signature of the Lydian ascension

spiced the harps of Greece. We have no music.

    Only words. And in them we read the music

         of revival, how it travelled from viol to
voice
through the hole each god left in passing.

       And the fear must have been particular,
the man alone and afraid. The hole was one hole, one night,
      gods left in passing,
  when the dissonance unnerved him, the signature tone
a *devil's tone*, he called it,

     and he must have been a man of power,

   and the music was a scripture. You can hear him still, if you read
as you listen, in the sweet erasures of the Lydian that rises
          in the middle,

as bodies do when they are young and sleeping. And if you listen enough,
a sharp gets less sharp, less offensive,
    older and younger in once instant.

     And whatever pain there
     grows familiar. And the dissonance unpins

  its nightgown. And the cotton falls.
         And the bitter cloud of ash
  lies down with the lamb
     and smoke in a field in Alabama.

The trumpet lies down with the daylight in its casket

        The lion with the lamb.
                              The harp with the harpist.

      The luggage with the luggage of the strangers.

            The plane with the shadow the grows in size to meet it

      The river lies down in a deeper river and the branches cast ashore.
            Childhood with the man who is its child.

Memory is its own memorial.
                    A name for the nameless.
                  An effacement, a sketch.

      Flesh lies down in the flesh, where the younger body goes.

Long ago I held a spear of ice
    so fierce it clung to my glove,

            and I was in the churchyard, alone.
How I got there, I cannot remember, where I was the moment before.

      My mother called my worried name. That much I know.
                                    Her voice
    lay down with the sun in the fathoms.

                And I, in silence, answered.

Beneath the bells and tremors of the tower, all the angels are kids,
                                              and all the children serious
                with ribbons and horns.

Between the saved and the damned is a wall on fire with saints
        and ornamental gold.
                                      The soprano is a boy.

        In the casket an uncle,
in his later years, a stranger,

                who pulled a coin one Easter from my ear.

                            I was told he was saved.
                            I was told no one knows.
                            If I was speechless, I do not remember.
Then. I do.
                    Out of nowhere, the silver.
                    I was breathless.
                    I was ice.

    I was heaven for a moment.

                        The astonished eye between his fingers.

        Staring back.

To each the silence
of impoverishment and that of plenty and the one still bell
            in a tower of bells.

And who can tell the one from the other,
            the music from the time of day,
            what it is our silence prays for.

Bury a man, and still
he speaks.
The silence of a chapel
                    after a service, it is a silence
         like no other.

        This much is common.

Bury a woman,
and still the complicity of trees in winter.

                    One man's comfort is another's affliction,
                  another's cathedral
        empties and fills and empties once again

                the silence of shock into that of wonder.

    The words of the widower into the speechless child
                    who will not be consoled.

Cold, sweet, and utterly clear,
                the silence of the untouched meal.

        Every plate a mirror, every mirror veiled.

The other side of lamentation is the shape it makes.

Me here, you there. And in the musical phrase,
                                a little breathing.

None of the tiresome pretense or maxims of appeasement.

The other side of music is always music and dark now

as the music to come. The music to come
                    ,
                        however named.

                    Is.   Nameless.

        The unborn child.
                            However named.

The other side of a photograph is always alive
            and dead and the river in it breathless
                .

                    Silent
                    as a river was
                            in the memorial hand
                    that held the camera.

Look hard enough, and you enter the space
            where the river, with its name, began.

These nights, I close my eyes, and the dust and branches

        on the shores of the border
                tumble through the chamber.

    Sometimes the sharp flash in the corner
        is the river.
                Sometimes the lens.

In a better dream, a boy carries his guitar

    over his head as he walks across the river.
                And where and when, however he plays,

   he gathers strangers on the road. Sometimes they know the words.

    Sometimes a fire at the center
              makes the makeshift gathering stare.

   In every eye of the circle, a particular fire.
      Smaller, deeper.

        In every flash in the corner. A river, a lens.

All that rises into heaven
dies. I see that now.

In a better dream,
the dust and branches on the shores of the border
                    tumble through the chamber.

III.

      Every voice an epitaph, and then a little tune
                              from the neighbor's yard.

I am learning to be two people, as voices are both voices
         and the music in them.
                         And music never promised
     a tomb, a home.
Only the narrow pleasure of departure.

I confess.
A voice is always two voices, one of which I do not hear,
and then I do. The music ends.

I have had that dream.

      I have worried the currency of words
      until all of the coins were headless.

      The cities empty. Heavens blind.

In the adolescence of my century,
                      the news is always late.

The storms from the gulf more furious and early.

More furious and early
         the crest and roar on the gulf horizon.

The girl who clings to her mother's skirt at the polling station
    is
        learning to be elsewhere.

    She looks one way, her mother another,
            and the curtains of the booths open and close,
        their black wings flutter
                      nowhere.

    If light comes late, then every eye is historical.

    Every dawn a dusk.
    Every line at the polling station a shadow of those
        before and the girl who stood there.

        I am searching
        for the planet that I stand on.

What I see I read, what I read I write, what I make
    opens a curtain on a garden that a stranger planted.

    Everywhere you look,
    an abstract of anonymous relations.

The vote, the earth, the layer of cloud on fire in the distance.

    I cast a shadow when I cast my vote, and the night,
        like fire, takes me
            in.

In his final year, my father grew tomatoes. He knelt
    a lot. He watered. He stared
    into the space where language left him.

    The fruit was green.
    No.
    Greener. *Beautiful*, I said, and still he stared.

    When he left, we said his name a lot.

    Then less and less. He scarred me.
    I will not lie. *Beautiful,*
    I said, because I was looking for a name and the stillness

    of relations.
    I was filling a hole. Me. Him.
The wind in the leaves.

    I was looking back from a time
where I too would be speechless.
    The earth green. No. Greener.

My father is beautiful there
    And the place he kneels a comfort.

    And the garden is on fire.

Every night
        he was given another life.
                Every morning
                          he gave it back to darkness.

He taught me to be nervous.
        And here we are. And therefore elsewhere.
                          Strangers in a garden.

My father listened poorly.
        He taught me to try hard.
        No. Harder. And then, quite suddenly, fatally,
                less.

I never saw him break until the language left him.

        Wind turned the leaves on the hill.
        And when I was alone, I stood on a cliff
            above my town.

        I saw in the distance
the acetylene and smoke, the winter of Los Angeles.

        I could have sworn it was a story,
        I was that alone. It was a story where nothing happens yet.

The book was blank. And lovely.
                      And then, as the night came on,

            a book.

One day

    the girl will cast her shadow
    across a hole in the garden

and find
    a man, a soldier, who fell to earth as angels fall and spring rain.

And he will grow in significance
    because he is nameless.

    She will place him on a table beside her bed and read.

    And her dream will have such fire in it,
    she will wake afraid and remember nothing.

    As if no one existed
    there. No soldier burned.

And at the breakfast table she will say nothing.

And her mother will worry. And the father who left them
will take his chair.

    I too am nowhere here. I take my chair.

I bury my father on a day in winter

    in a park that blooms all year.

I am searching my ballot for the nameless.

         She is out there, in there,
   I call her *nameless*,
       but I am thinking of a man
  without a home, and I know:
         this is just one example.

I am searching my ballot for a woman

   without registration, and in the distance,
   bells toll for time alone.

        I am searching the bells
  for a space to sign,

when my wife tells me
     they talked G-d at temple, He who has no name.
       He is just that essential.

She who has no circumference, no core.
  She is just that vital.

  She the field through which the blades
  of sparrows rise.

  She the blade and the sparrow.
  The song torn from the sparrow's throat.

  She who has no vote.

  She the stainless spires of the financial district.
  The clear green scent beneath the underpass at dawn.

The light that leaves the body in the morning,
                         it bears no signature, no news,

and the man who wakes
            thinks of free coffee at the mission.

       A heaven in a sermon where we all have names.
                              And none of us have ballots.

God loves you,
       she whose breath is this ghost in the cold,

       whose shadow
             is every shadow grown long
             at dawn, and then—in the rising smoke
             and progress of the sun—compressed.

I woke once to a club called heaven without any members.

       It was a club on fire in the woods
       and people warmed their hands there.
       I was small and happy.
       So strong my joy, I nearly disappeared.

When I cast my vote, I become just that tiny, abstract, lost and essential.

       Light as prayer.
       And then I step through the ghost of mist
                       across the parking lot.

Somewhere I left a car. My car. And I stand still a moment.

       Like a bust of someone dead and important.

White in the white
                              of the lost republic.

When I gather what the nameless left,
    I am speechless.
                           They who poured
    into this warm belated body, this world,

        as I poured into them to see if we made progress.

      As a boy, I buried things.
A jar of coins, a toy soldier, the jokers of a deck.

        I drew a map with an x
                for my imagined reader,

    my child.
    And what I buried increased in significance

        because I buried it.

Like wind buried in the word *wind,*
      and word and wind, in a still context of winter,

    will never be the same.

                It could have been most any
        otherwise
    meaningless thing.

            A bee, a ticket, a box of matches.

I read it in an old book:

          the word *thank* is to *think*,

     as *song* is to *sing*.

      It sounded like a song to me.

Like a bird repeating its figure in air, and then the turn.

  The buried words,

      their insistence is surprising.

      Their coins are heads lost to the hands

      of the many.

         The word *think*

is to *life*, as *life* is to the dying.

     Daylight falls through the trees and the gardens

        and the birds that eat them.

            And yet, and yet,

  they sing.

Compulsion must have something in it

        that is new.

        Something lost.

  Some greed that believes it is *good.* The host of greed that is always dying.

    The host of belief.

The treasures of my yard are down there still.

       In the fire and the cloud and broken earth

      I always thought

        preserved them.

IV.

I carry a face

>	a step ahead
>	and the years and dust and wind in the branches
>	have beaten the shield
>	and I know one day it will crumble
>	beneath the weather,
>
>	it will expose the always younger
>	idea behind,
>	and the flock of swallows will scatter,
>	the latch will fly
>	on a suitcase of wind,
>
>	and those I love will fold their black umbrellas
>	and step into the cars,
>
>	well, not all of them of course,
>
>	they will drive to their separate homes
>	and check the mail,
>	lower the little red flag on its box
>	with a creak,
>
>	and step inside
>	where dust and wind from the desert margins of Los
Angeles
>	can, if
summoned, find them.

And if one I knew and loved should feed
the fire, drink the light,
if my eyes and robe should bear
the revenant smoke,
unaware,

if one whose name I am
beginning
to forget leans in a little closer,

I will think of something
my cat once said,

how *the subject does not belong in the world:*
rather he is
the limit of a world.

And then he will lick his leg.
He will look at me.

Ashes will fall.

He licks his leg once more.

    And I will wonder
    if
    he

    noted the

    shift from *the* world to *a*
    makes
    the whole ball of yarn unravel.

This is a story where you meet a face
        at the opening
        and realize you never really looked
        there.
        The story never looked.

    It began with a shield
    whose only opening was death.

    A part of me is cat,
    that cat in particular.

    Half the time
    I cannot know what my cat is saying.

Is the cry a cry
for a face, a pat,
a waiter
in the vast cruel restaurant of nature,
versus what these features
say,

what the face and flesh behind it
understands,

what it questions, sees,
or
otherwise bestows.

Is it just me
or do you hear him.

When the answer cannot be put in words, neither can the question be put in words.

And then my cat added, *mrgnow.*

Which is a quote from great classic of Irish literature.

And everything he said after that felt a little political. Classical.

~~When~~ the answer cannot be ~~put in words, neither can~~ the question ~~be put in words.~~

~~When the answer cannot be put in words,~~ neither can the question be put in words.

And so I asked,

How does that melody go?

The song
where the brother
holds the receiver to the father's mouth
and I am far away
and say something awkward
about how I feel, and I hear him breathing
into the phone
as if he carried some great burden, some message,
he is hoping to lay down.

What we cannot speak about we must pass over in silence,

                                                said the silence.

And then the whole sentence unraveled
                into music.
                              And the silence was a part.

      The part where the singer breathes.

~~What~~ we ~~cannot speak about we must pass over~~ in silence.

~~What we cannot speak about~~ we must pass over ~~in silence.~~

~~What we cannot speak about~~ we must pass over ~~in silence.~~

What we cannot speak ~~about~~ we must ~~pass over in silence,~~

_____

Look at me.
My dreams say in the morning.
                But when I answer,
                I am dead to them.

My voice sounds more and more

        like my father's.

        My silence less and less.

V.

    The passports of the tombstones
    have all been dated, stamped,

    abandoned. The rain shivers through. The sky goes clear.

        Flowers, if there are flowers,
                fresh-cut as the names they lie on,
they last a week or two
            before they join the clippings of the morning.

        The stone angels have all gone blind,
    and those who talk to them speak of regret, reunion, something
    in the news.
            Those whose hearts are stones that listen.

When I was a boy, I played alone
    with matches in the garden,

            and the little souls of the ants were at my mercy.
        I was more afraid than I knew

of solitude and worse. Its absence. I was cruel.

    And then more sweetly miserable.

I was powerless
    to stop. I thought. Better to say I was a stranger
        to my power. I was the abandoned field
in a pastoral.

        And I stared transfixed into the fire.

As a child I learned and forgot and learned again
   everything

            has a name, save one.
   G-d, the nameless, made it so.

   Every man with his face in the warm cloud above his cup.

And I know: *everything*
    is
    a name already
    and so bereft of its nameless home.

   Among the many, there is one who drinks my dollar
   and the one who does not,

   and one who in her cold flesh wakes
   to the dream of a republic.

       God loved me as a child.

   Every dawn I cast my shadow to the shadows.

And, bidden or unbidden, my silhouette returns.

       Like a child, it clings.

          As the day grows old.

Bidden or unbidden, God abideth. So says the tomb

    of a Swiss in the Latin of a Dutchman,
                                          cribbed in turn
    from an unnamed Greek.

    Bidden or unbidden,

the mist above the Allegheny
rises through the fathoms and just keeps rising.

    One man's comfort is another's paranoia.
    One man's God, a sheriff. Or another, a nurse.

            One man's forsaken conscience
    returns, and he knows
    his drinking is a problem, and so he drinks.

    And bidden or unbidden,
    the Allegheny in the rainy season tears a tree from shore.

The dead are talking under us, the water falling.
    We know they are not talking really, and so they talk.

And the wheel of the rose cart crackles
                                through the leaves.

Bidden or unbidden, dream visits the sleepless man,
    and so he wakes.

    And so he wakes again.

    And when he looks at you, he sees a mist
    and the river with its branches borne downstream.

    The dead are talking over him.

    Named or nameless, they are flashing through the water,
as water,
        somewhere, flashes through the form it takes.

The Allegheny and the rain and the ache of mist
        in the morning, they fall across the threshold
        into the grave of many

    that is the name of each.

Form flashes through form as hunger flashes through a brain.
    Wine through the laughter.
        Laughter through the blood.

    Light flashes through the ice it breaks.
    I swear.

    And the oceans rise.

I have a friend who lost the memory of a year from his childhood,

    and he just kept losing it.
    He just kept looking

    through the drinking glass, through the downpour blur
        in the barroom mirror.

    The Allegheny and the rain and the chain-link
    shiver
    in the stream, the trailing pattern of the branch,

    they score the eye, the way a pen scores the page.

    And some days I feel lighter, larger, more broken
    open.
    I see and therefore read and therefore write and carve

    a passage, and sometimes it closes
    behind, and every one I know is waiting

    on earth. I erase the words,
    I have a friend, and the space is dawn eating into dream.

    Some wounds get large when you kneel to wash them.

The smell of smoke and roses in a bar,
                the water in the delirious eye,
                              the ice of the laugh that makes it shine.

                When I think of a friend, I think of this, this
face and the river that pulls it
                over. I think,

        The Future of an Illusion was his favorite book,
        and I loved him,
        he who was mean and generous

and loved to read. And one day in bed, his author came to him

            and said, I know. Compulsion is water
                    pushing water from its path,
                                and the path grows deep.

            Sometimes god is a nurse, sometimes a sheriff,
            but you, you are free.

You with your book in your hands, your open grave.

        Free as a river in the rainy season,
a scar of light in the current

                      no wounded eye recalls.

To every infant, the daze of arrival.
>							The roses stupefied, bobbing on their stems.

The un-struck bell the one clear shape
>							in a photo-blur of bells.

The mobile of moons above the cradle is a memory
>							so deep it is no memory to me.

But there it is.
The breath in the body.

>			The air that hides in the voice around it.
>			The earth in the shroud.
>			The future in the fire that burns the shroud away.

>			Today I learned a new word. *Post-truth.*
>			The silence of noise.

In the adolescence of the new century,
>	the earth is the one clear bell in a blur of bells.

The silence of night is like no other.
>							The slate on which a myth is written.

>		Clear as dreams to the sleepless
>							who wait in turn to read them.

There is the silence of abundance and that of abandon,

    and bidden or unbidden,
    they are bound
    for some dark passage in the wilderness.

    The silence of permission lies down deeper and deeper
    on the silence of a child,

        and so he is a child still.

There is the silence of earth unlike no other.

      The silence of a name

          lies down on the silence of bronze.

      And they are never one thing
      only.
              The smoke over the Allegheny
    lies down on the water,
    and those who see it read it, write it.

The earth on fire, it consecrates
                a language.
                Out of nowhere,
    this gift. A little nowhere in it still
        I call gratitude. A little fall

        from pride.

Out of nothing, the fire of affluence and that of ruin.
    The light of understanding
               and that of understanding coming
               to a face.

       What I do not know I must pass through
       in silence.

       Influence. I came from *this*,
       under *this*,
       me, my river, my friend,

from a time when earth was a torrent,

       a god,
       her name a branch that tore the river open.

Call this chair a c-r. Table, t-e. Wine, w-e.
Each, a follower.

Every borderland, breached.

       And what pours through is blood and muscle
       and the music of a thousand
       tongues.

             A gift how deep
the muscle goes.
The host. Me here. Your breathing there.

       The root in the throat and farther, darker.

             There is no language
                          but this.

ACKNOWLEDGMENTS

Sections of this book have appeared in *The Colorado Review, Denver Quarterly, Interim, Narrative, New American Writing, Plume, The Public Poetry Prize Anthology, Southern Humanities Review, Volt,* and *Witness.*

About the Author

Bruce Bond is the author of twenty-five books including, most recently, *Immanent Distance: Poetry and the Metaphysics of the Near at Hand* (U of MI, 2015), *Black Anthem* (Tampa Review Prize, U of Tampa, 2016), *Gold Bee* (Helen C. Smith Award, Crab Orchard Award, SIU Press, 2016), *Sacrum* (Four Way, 2017), *Blackout Starlight: New and Selected Poems 1997-2015* (L.E. Phillabaum Award, LSU, 2017), *Rise and Fall of the Lesser Sun Gods* (Elixir Book Prize, Elixir Press, 2018), *Dear Reader* (Free Verse Editions, 2018), *Frankenstein's Children* (Lost Horse, 2018), *Plurality and the Poetics of Self* (Palgrave, 2019), and *Words Written Against the Walls of the City* (LSU, 2019). Presently he is a Regents Professor of English at the University of North Texas.

Photograph of the author by Nicki Cohen.
Used by permission.

FREE VERSE EDITIONS

Edited by Jon Thompson

13 ways of happily by Emily Carr
& in Open, Marvel by Felicia Zamora
Alias by Eric Pankey
At Your Feet (A Teus Pés) by Ana Cristina César, edited by Katrina Dodson, translated by Brenda Hillman and Helen Hillman
Bari's Love Song by Kang Eun-Gyo, translated by Chung Eun-Gwi
Between the Twilight and the Sky by Jennie Neighbors
Blood Orbits by Ger Killeen
The Bodies by Christopher Sindt
The Book of Isaac by Aidan Semmens
The Calling by Bruce Bond
Canticle of the Night Path by Jennifer Atkinson
Child in the Road by Cindy Savett
Condominium of the Flesh by Valerio Magrelli, translated by Clarissa Botsford
Contrapuntal by Christopher Kondrich
Country Album by James Capozzi
The Curiosities by Brittany Perham
Current by Lisa Fishman
Day In, Day Out by Simon Smith
Dear Reader by Bruce Bond
Dismantling the Angel by Eric Pankey
Divination Machine by F. Daniel Rzicznek
Elsewhere, That Small by Monica Berlin
Empire by Tracy Zeman
Erros by Morgan Lucas Schuldt
Fifteen Seconds without Sorrow by Shim Bo-Seon, translated by Chung Eun-Gwi and Brother Anthony of Taizé
The Forever Notes by Ethel Rackin
The Flying House by Dawn-Michelle Baude
Go On by Ethel Rackin
Instances: Selected Poems by Jeongrye Choi, translated by Brenda Hillman, Wayne de Fremery, & Jeongrye Choi
The Magnetic Brackets by Jesús Losada, translated by Michael Smith & Luis Ingelmo
Man Praying by Donald Platt
A Map of Faring by Peter Riley
The Miraculous Courageous by Josh Booton

Mirrorforms by Peter Kline
No Shape Bends the River So Long by Monica Berlin & Beth Marzoni
Not into the Blossoms and Not into the Air by Elizabeth Jacobson
Overyellow, by Nicolas Pesquès, translated by Cole Swensen
Physis by Nicolas Pesquès, translated by Cole Swensen
Pilgrimage Suites by Derek Gromadzki
Pilgrimly by Siobhán Scarry
Poems from above the Hill & Selected Work by Ashur Etwebi, translated by Brenda Hillman & Diallah Haidar
The Prison Poems by Miguel Hernández, translated by Michael Smith
Puppet Wardrobe by Daniel Tiffany
Quarry by Carolyn Guinzio
remanence by Boyer Rickel
Republic of Song by Kelvin Corcoran
Rumor by Elizabeth Robinson
Settlers by F. Daniel Rzicznek
Signs Following by Ger Killeen
Small Sillion by Joshua McKinney
Split the Crow by Sarah Sousa
Spine by Carolyn Guinzio
Spool by Matthew Cooperman
Summoned by Guillevic, trans. by Monique Chefdor & Stella Harvey
Sunshine Wound by L. S. Klatt
System and Population by Christopher Sindt
These Beautiful Limits by Thomas Lisk
They Who Saw the Deep by Geraldine Monk
The Thinking Eye by Jennifer Atkinson
This History That Just Happened by Hannah Craig
An Unchanging Blue: Selected Poems 1962–1975 by Rolf Dieter Brinkmann, translated by Mark Terrill
Under the Quick by Molly Bendall
Verge by Morgan Lucas Schuldt
The Wash by Adam Clay
We'll See by Georges Godeau, translated by Kathleen McGookey
What Stillness Illuminated by Yermiyahu Ahron Taub
Winter Journey [Viaggio d'inverno] by Attilio Bertolucci, translated by Nicholas Benson
Wonder Rooms by Allison Funk

www.ingramcontent.com/pod-product-compliance
Lightning Source LLC
LaVergne TN
LVHW041309080426
835510LV00009B/917